I have worked with children, adolescents and adults all with varying disabilities.

My heart has been invested in every single one of them, and to them, I dedicate this book.

-NM

To my amazing friends, family, colleagues and my husband, Anthony.

Your support has been abounding. Thank you.

Oh, and thanks to Henry, my furry little pal for inspiring me.

ISBN-13: 978-1523694822

ISBN-10: 1523694823

CreateSpace Independent Publishing Platform

My Friend Henry

Written by Nicole Marie Milea

Illustrated by Juliana Barcia

This is my friend, Henry.

My friend Henry is fluffy and furry and snuggly, too.

He doesn't look very much like me at all.

Are you fluffy or furry?

Oh well, I bet you're snuggly though.

My friend Henry doesn't speak like I speak, he squeaks.
Sometimes it's a LOUD squeak, sometimes it's a *low* squeak.

I don't need him to speak how I speak to know when he is sad or sleepy or happy or mad, I can sometimes just tell by the way he acts.

Do you speak "squeak"?

I didn't think so.

What is your favorite food?

My friend Henry LOVES hay, hay is kind of like grass.

He loves to chew it and chew it and chew it.

Sometimes he eats raisins and peanuts and even potato chips;

I like those foods.

I don't eat hay though, but that's okay.

My friend Henry LOVES to run and run and run on his wheel.
I'd rather dance or play kickball or go swimming; but not Henry.

Henry LOVES his wheel.

Sometimes while Henry runs and runs and runs, I go into his
room and I dance and dance and dance.

I'm not a very good dancer, but Henry doesn't seem to mind.

After all that running and running and running my friend Henry gets very, very sleepy.

Henry needs it to be quiet and peaceful and dark to fall asleep so I do my very, very best to not make too much noise or turn on the lights.

Apparently I like naps just as much as Henry does. When it's all quiet... and peaceful... and dark... I get very, very sleepy too...

...ZzzzzZzzzzzZzzzzz

BOOM!

Did that scare you?

My friend Henry gets scared by loud noises too.

He runs away to hide somewhere that makes him feel safe.

A hug afterwards usually helps.

I'll always give Henry a hug if I know it makes him feel better.

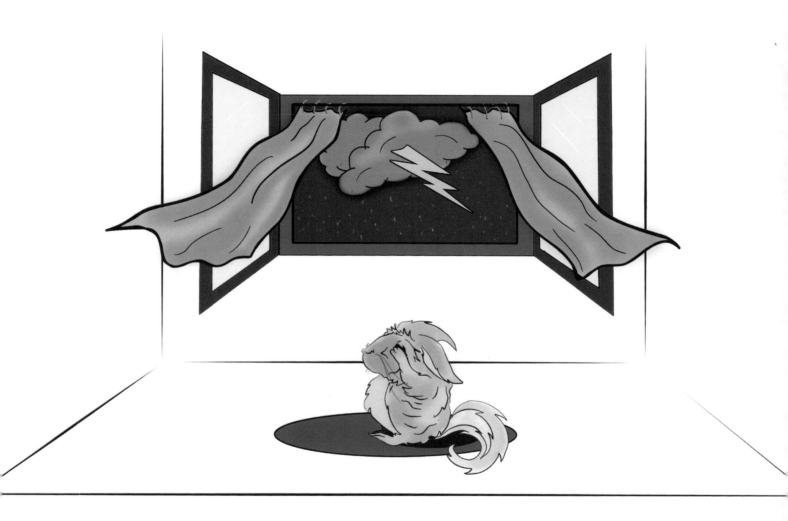

My friend Henry is soooo curious.

Henry always wants to play downstairs in the basement;

I'm sooo scared of the basement.

It's dark and spooky and creepy and creaky...

Henry's hands and feet don't work like mine; sometimes he needs my help when he wants to explore new things.

Henry is so brave, he helps me feel brave.

Into the basement we go!

We help each other, that's what friends do.

My friend Henry isn't very much like me.

And that's okay.

Henry doesn't judge my not so good dancing.

I don't have fluff or fur or speak "squeak" or eat hay or
like dark and spooky and creepy and creaky basements.

But, I do like naps.

And that's enough.

Because Henry is my friend.

ABOUT THE AUTHOR

Nicole Marie Milea is a Special Education Teacher from Staten Island, New York. She has spent a dedicated career teaching, supporting and learning from those individuals with varying disabilities. Having worked with individuals of varying ages, her passion for what she does extends well beyond the classroom; from early-intervention, providing therapy to children in their homes to managing an adult group home. Nicole is a strong advocate for disabilities awareness of all kinds and plans to continue working hard in bringing further awareness to the cause.

Different is **not** less.

My friend Henry is intended to be utilized as a platform in bringing

acceptance of differences in friendships to the world of disabilities awareness.

As a community we need to work together in inspiring our youth to see the

ABILITY within the dis[**ability**].